COLLECTED WORKS

20 08 16

D0390109

Volume 98 of the Yale Series of Younger Poets

FOR BARBARA —

THANK YOU FOR BEING

HERE, IN THE ART.

pete

the cuckoo

peter streckfus

Foreword by Louise Glück

yale university press   new haven and london

Published with assistance from the Kingsley Trust Association Publication
Fund established by the Scroll and Key Society of Yale College.

Designed by Sonia Shannon
Set in Bulmer type with Futura display
by Tseng Information Systems.
Printed in the United States of America.

Library of Congress Cataloging-in-Publication Data
Streckfus, Peter.
The cuckoo / Peter Streckfus ; foreword by Louise Glück.
       p.   cm. — (The Yale series of younger poets ; v. 98)
ISBN 978-0-300-10272-7
I. Title.   II. Series.
PS3619.T745C83   2004
811'.6 — dc22   2003063391

A catalogue record for this book is available from the British Library.

The paper in this book meets the guidelines for permanence and durability
of the Committee on Production Guidelines for Book Longevity of the
Council on Library Resources.

bulluc sterteth bucke verteth

Turn the head of your horse
sideways across the field
to let me hear
the cry hototogisu.
—Matsuo Basho

Contents

Foreword

The case for nonsense is not the same as the case against meaning.
It belongs, in literature, to the holy fool and cryptic sprite; in religion,
to the visionary or the seer; in philosophy, to the Sphinx and the Zen
master. It is animated not by an objection to meaning, which it intends
and reveres, but by a refusal of the restrictive governing of meaning
by will and logic. For the tools of reason, it substitutes the resources
of magic; against the rigidity of the absolute, it suggests the hypnotic
power of the evanescent; for narrative, it offers collage or prism; for
conclusion, hypothesis.

    Such art asks, inevitably, a kind of consent of the reader. Or,
in Peter Streckfus's unforgettable first book, more active cooperation:
what is transacted here between poet and reader has less to do with
the reader's being convinced by elegant or passionate argument, and
more to do with seduction. And the instrument of our seduction, for
once, is not charm but mesmerizing beauty:

> Great Banquet in Heaven; you see,
> illustrious, plentiful, a forest, and a library kept
> in its understory,

pages and pages of paper for the bureaucrat or scholar,
a woman at the edge of a field bounding on the forest,
an umbrella yellow in her right hand,
her fingernails of jade,
on her finger a worn ring of five-color gold;

a cuckoo
and a cowbird about their usurpations,
and (such were the animals present)
white tailed deer, the flags of their white tails
seen out over whatever water that is.

Why is there a woman and not a man? Why is there not a child?
And what has this to do with heaven?
Because you are the man, a slender penis between your legs.
Of this we shall speak more later.

It would all fail, of course, the effect of the spell dissipate, were
the universe of this art less profoundly original, less richly imagined.
An atmosphere of luminous high-mindedness suffuses Streckfus's
poems—high-mindedness not in any sense constricting or pedantic or
puritanical. Nonsense and mystery are not substitutes for truth; they
are its consorts, engaged with it in perpetual dialogue. And the realm
in which such dialogue occurs lists among its attributes purity and, to
some extent, unworldliness.

The actual and the fantastic, the historical and the imaginary do
not so much collide as interweave; Streckfus uses realities piecemeal,
his phenomenal ear alert to continuities. Like Frank Bidart, he uses, to
his own ends, materials from existing sources. He shares with Bidart
a feeling, too, for ritual; there, for the moment, resemblance ends.
Streckfus's characteristic mode is allegory or parable; his characteris-
tic metaphor, the journey. (Equally characteristic is his reluctance to
specify, or his disinterest in, a journey's object or purpose, as though
the need that there be a journey precedes any particular catalyst.)
What survives of the journey is not the dramatic arc of narrative but

rather archetypal form, a kind of infinite passage, neither driven nor haunted. Streckfus's odd compressed epics, like "Event," like "The Organum," seem almost tonal analyses of narrative, so eerily exact as to compel precisely as a story would, though there is no story, merely the story's shape and cadence—no one, I think, has quite discerned the template in this manner. More remarkable is how much feeling survives: one wouldn't expect heartbreak to be among the effects of such a method, but it is.

Nor would it seem the province of this voice, a term that seems curiously inadequate or inappropriate to so disembodied an instrument. Calm, floating, speaking sometimes in the manner of the ancient soul, sometimes as the initiate: it is a voice from which all turbulence has been expelled, leaving a tenderly attentive detachment. And yet it can turn, for all its uncanny remoteness, stricken, ecstatic. Nothing in contemporary poetry sounds like the ravishing end of "Event":

> Because I'd seen them so often come here
> to the most remote part of the garden and rub the centers
>
> of their bodies together beneath their changing petals,
> I considered them part of my own. And they considered me the same
>
> coming to me as they did on this day.
> They took one of my fruit and gave it to her, and then taking my
>
> branch and stripping it of all its leaves,
> and stripping her garments, they beat her with my branch,
>
> the white flesh of my fruit running through her fisted hand until it
> held only my seed.
>
> If it is true, as the lemons say, that he is a god, then this must
> be the way it is done. I saw her stiffen, from blossom to dead

and pregnant fruit, the white flesh almost beaten away, her
body rolled to a ball.

I saw a kind of shell within her open, its contents taken by the wind.
Ah, so this is how they are borne.

By positioning his speaker in a tree, Streckfus has managed to
transcribe the great mystery: a soul passes from its body into air; the
human species is carried off like a seed. The tree, I think, wishes to
learn how it is done, this being human, since it has been the tool of
a human act, an act in this case murderous. This is a world of trans-
formations, mutations, the physical transformed to the spiritual and
back again. The fluid long poems move in shapely scenes and lyric
episodes, in puzzle pieces: ideas, phrases, figures recur, appearing
and disappearing. Streckfus's predilection for anachronism intensifies
the impression—time becomes, in this poetry, a series of overlap-
ping transparencies; we are meant, I think, to sense what might be
called eternal shapes, as though, if it were possible to move back far
enough from transience and change, one would see, clearly, the large
recurrences.

Peter Streckfus's quiet authority is uncommon in contemporary
poetry, especially uncommon in one so young. We expect, I think,
other strengths: intensity, technical virtuosity. Or delicacy, the perfec-
tion of the small thing. Not this confident serene mastery, this soaring,
Streckfus's strangely distant intimacy and peculiar pageantry: he lives
deeply in imagination; the quotidian, the social, impinge very little.
And the constructs of that imagination owe their scale to the breadth
of Streckfus's sources; he seems, often, like a seer raised in the world
of George Lucas.

He is not afraid of grandeur. He is willing, like the cuckoo, to
appropriate; he borrows his nests. And his evasions seem purposeful
and necessary, an enactment of his refusal of the confinements of sense
and firm conclusion—doors do not close in this poetry, rooms are not
sealed off. And yet he dignifies a reader's need for finality, for clear

answers, for solid, verifiable ground. Though he will not accommo-
date that need, his acknowledgment of it results in solicitude, a gentle
invitation to move beyond the known, the secure:

Let me tell you a story. A woman farmer had two she-goats . . .

And the story proceeds, in the leisurely fashion of a fairy tale, a bed-
time story:

Springs before she left off milking,
she always had a few kids

hopping in the yard like cupids.
The billy she penned separately so the milk wouldn't taste like sex.
Then, death appeared with the rustic

twittering of juncos, the place a shambles, the tree rats

deep in the brush.

I know nothing

of goats. I apologize beforehand that they become tangled in
my story. The billy will wish it'd never had horns,

its whole life spent
licking its own penis and scratching those castles on its head
as if they were boils that needed lancing;

the she-goats will be in chains, put on a run by a well meaning city-
man. . . .

A parable, an allegory, whose title, "Why I Slept with Him," invites
the reader to expect certain satisfactions. But for Streckfus, that is
the problem, that expectation of satisfaction, of the single answer.
To know how it felt to be the other? Because there was no choice?
Perhaps, perhaps not:

> . . . See? How he pulls
the black one's leg from the chain about the little

> one's neck in the moon light? And how, understanding goats as
social animals, he will inevitably run them

> > out the next day?

And then it is the next day; the imagination draws confidence from accurate prediction:

> . . . Let's go down and untangle them.
> > We'll take their places.
> Here he is with his well meaning hands.
> The pupils of our eyes are sliced off at the top and the bottom
> and we've lost our voices. Have you ever seen how sad
> > a goat's eyes are? Look into mine.

The poem ends elusively, in a teasing evasion: it works like a riddle — you will want an answer, a decision, it says; I will give you the clues from which response may be inferred.

It is a move this poet understands deeply. Refusals and evasions that, in a lesser artist, would seem irritating or tricky seem, in Streckfus, subtle instruction: in tolerance of ambiguity and irresolution, in patience. The wish for an answer, like the wish for stability, is at bottom a wish for self-deception; Streckfus will not honor it.

In that sense, he is something of a moralist. Unmistakably, he is a seeker, his quests and journeys unlike any I have encountered. The reader is less required than invited. And how formidable the delight of accepting, how rare the adventure:

> Here is a wall. The strange empty space above the wall . . . what is it
> for? Here, a little boat, a canopy of silver plastic rattling above it.

> Listen to the babe-scare cry of the wind. . . .

And then:

> There's no place for that weapon here. Come on now, you have no
> choice. Trust me.
>
> I'll speak nonsense. You speak truth. We'll see what comes of it.

Louise Glück

Acknowledgments

Grateful acknowledgment is made to the editors of the following publications where these poems, sometimes in previous forms, first found readers: *Beloit Poetry Journal:* "Why I Slept with Him" and "After Words"; *Natural Bridge:* "Model of a Tree Growing in the Path of a Spiral" and "The Celery Cutters' Song"; *Phoebe:* "When Ronald Reagan Was a Boy," "The Carpenter," and "Death and a Fig"; *Pleiades:* "The Bird," "The Dung Pile," and "Retreat"; *Slope:* "Event" and "Journey to the West."

I thank Louise Glück, from whose tireless dedication this book has benefited, and my teachers, Jennifer Atkinson, Carolyn Forché, Peter Klappert, Eric Pankey, and Susan Tichy, who have supported and guided me along the way. Further gratitude to Ilya Kaminsky, Leonard and Carol Nathan, Tobin O'Donnell; Salt Creek Farm and Potomac Vegetable Farms, where I lived and worked while many of these poems were first composed; and, with the profoundest wonder and love, to Bird.

PART I

The English

Crusoe: A bee.

Friday: Bee?

C: Aye, a bee.

F: Bee . . .

C: Aye.

later . . .

C: City.

F: Cee Dee

C: City.

Journey to the West

In the beginning of the period known as the T'ang, Hsüan-tsang
     quietly joined
a body of itinerant bicycle merchants and set off on that pilgrimage
to learn for certain whether all or part of humanity can attain
     Buddhahood.
At customs, they posed as a nongovernmental organization (NGO),

avoiding taxes. Marketing, they rang the triangles of the bicycle
frames
as if bells to demonstrate the air-like quality of their wares, and
     laced the spokes
with colored papers, or turned the handlebars upside down, if it
     reflected the tastes
of the province. Nights, they slept beneath the trucks to protect
     their goods. Settled in his place

among them, staring at the constellations of the great vehicle above
     him—
king pin, leaf springs, bushing—without knowing what he saw, he
     fell asleep, hand cupped
over his genitals. How was he to know his quest for the ineffable
would be turned into the hundred-chaptered tale of a man-sized
     gibbon and his golden-

hooped iron rod, a tale that leads our pilgrim over those snow-
     toothed mountains with no mention
of the merchants, nor Tai-tsung's imperial forbiddance of the
     journey through the unguarded frontier?
Tai-tsung, who traveled that region in the safer days of his youth,
     knowing it filled

with more than civet and deer, bid our pilgrim to remain in the Pure
    Land cloister

of Lo-Yang. Tai-tsung, emperor, nescient of the blossom of this
    story, who dreamed
of a man gazing east so long he finally discerned a still figure —
the back of his own head. While Hsüan-tsang, wakened from sleep,
    continued on his way,
"wary to the mind's distinctions, senses guarded."

Memories Are Nothing, Today Is Important

Trust the moth that flutters in your shirt. Its branch
is nearby. Secondly, you must fix your guitar.
For this you would need knife, glue and string. The hand
is like the head—keep the fingers moving or they stiffen.
You are a fisherman. Cast from the edge of this pond
your hook, snelled to this line with a bit of gut. Cleave
the water below. Lastly, you must name the lights
that line your constellation—how else can you eat?
Call a star *work*, call another cardinal light
my house. You may name the others. Surrounded
by these points, you must keep the balance, lively fish
in this pond of stars, cleaving the waters below.

Retreat

i

Three things I require, and the first is fruit.
Shad, you will call it, or, then, June berry.
The indigens who prize its pliant limbs
as shafts for their missiles call it Saskatoon.

Though I came with good root stock, my trials
will not take. The seed, if and when you send
it, I pray, will do, or I must ask
for soil. The griefs of latitude, I tell you,

are slight. In the gardens of the Ozzette,
I first ate the food they call pemmican,
the black pome and its almondine seeds ground
in the rendered lard of bear and salmon

rended and dried — this cake shall constitute
my one sustenance. Three years hence,

I will send you word for the fat and fish.

ii

An-bar, the fire from the heavens,
Sumerian name for iron, fell
from the darkness in my mind, its locks of dust
cracked, three days prior to this morning's letter.

Since that time, I have been at work, adze
of a forty penny nail in hand,
turning my island before the augur
of harvest depletes me of both warmth and mettle.

I heard a thunder, though the sky was clear.
A flag of smoke at half a league's distance.
There, ranging from a walnut's size
to that of a pea, near a small crater,

a celestial metal in fragments
that even the brine could not corrupt.

Three things to despise, and the first is rust.

Encephalitis

If your drop of lemon juice leaves the lemon in your hand and the oyster doesn't wriggle upon being touched by the juice of the lemon you should not eat it for the oyster is not whole in its mind.

The Dung Pile

The varied voices of crows rose and fell. As I lay in the grass, dark-
   eyed juncos flew down beside me,

flittering and twittering, and gleaned the mustard seed fallen onto
   my body. Their black beads and death hoods.

Their white coat tails. I whispered to them: Surely it is you who
   make the honey of which the Berber speak,

honey which they secret from your nest in the dreamy hours of the
   haze, lining their throats each morning

as if with a paste of fire ant stings,

or do you make the mists which tangle into clouds through the
   mountains

to the south of ranches? They continued to eat from me. One picked
   out an oat seed, another, a blade of bluestem.

PART II

Ode

The most beautiful thing in my life today. A nut brown flea
floating in the middle of a lake underlain with white flowers.

My bowl of tea.

The armor glistens, its equine head and legs stammer
in this new element, knocked by arrow or hammer

that fatal moment in the field.

Event

I would teach you what they've done
to me had I arms to teach it
and a voice to keep silent.
Your sweetness brought me to this.
But why has my destiny
placed me inside your sickening
bole? And why do you drop your
fruit at my dead body's feet?

Great Banquet in Heaven; you see,
illustrious, plentiful, a forest, and a library kept
in its understory,

      pages and pages of paper for the bureaucrat or scholar;
a woman at the edge of a field bounding on the forest,
an umbrella yellow in her right hand,
her fingernails of jade,
on her finger a worn ring of five-color gold;

          a cuckoo
and a cowbird about their usurpations,
and (such were the animals present)
white tailed deer, the flags of their white tails
seen out over whatever water that is.

Why is there a woman and not a man? Why is there not a child?
   And what has this to do with heaven?
Because you are the man, a slender penis between your legs.
Of this we shall speak more later.

Trees and mown grass as far as the eye can see,
or his mother's hand pointing to the hillscape
as in a painting of the late Gothic period,
                              which to her love's an allegorie,

her finger pointing to the hills before Johnson City on Hwy. 71,
                              the hills like the armored heart, armadillo,

or, elsewhere, the bloated limbs of the wuchack (woodchuck)
on the road, the hills crowned in fine hair and nails like that,

               overrun and dependent on the road for their beauty.

In retired life, the president hears only the birds
                              who have eaten his peaches for him.

High winds do not last all morning.
Ruling the country is like cooking a small fish.

Inner light relumed. Or livestock sacrificed.
Not seeing desirable things. Or cowing.

Washed. Or unkempt and without hindrance.
The gold-hooped nature. Or this one now aims to kill!

Sky astray, the president's old foe evades his parry,
but using his lance with difficulty, he halts the monkey's rod.

Beyond the low bridge, willows
          to untangle these in the monkey of the mind.

Therefore the sage goes about doing nothing (silence)
And in thirty-six heavens twenty picking monkeys march homeward.

No wind, the sage says, is the president's wind.
A tractor begins a circle in the grass, off path,

                                        its engine lugging—
On the tractor in the field of heaven, asleep for a moment,

            he dreams another man's dream, steeped in another time,

                                        a still figure. . . .
Passing along the fence, and then
through its broken spine, he continues
toward the porch. "Let me have some lunch first.

    Then I'll wage contest with you," he repeats to himself,
tasting, within, a porridge of oats mixed with leek,
"or maybe," with sour milk, raisins and seeds,
stale tea. The monkey's voice: "Shiftless.

        You want to be a hero? Consider old Monkey, imprisoned below
the mountain without even a drop of water.
Which hero needs to eat after fighting half a day?"

The remnants of this morning's peach (sweep
away the ants) and then a fresh one.

Garden around the basilica and all I have there;
columbine my special favorite, it's spaceship-like;

too many needs, and tired of talking about the light—
Once, in a cabinet meeting, Ron Reagan, when asked of what he
was thinking, simply moved closer
                         and said, "Shhh."

The spur of its petals.

The jade white moth brows, eager to have the jade green cabbage,
        float by.

Why is there a woman and not a man? Why is there not a child?
Great banquet in Heaven, you see
                            how little there is to offer?

The woman at the edge of the field is the center of his
story: an emperor's.

The president's most loved was whipped to death with the branch of
a litchee. A pause in our journey,
                      Pilgrim Sun, fiery monkey of
stone that these our stories orbit, does a quick cloud somersault and
passes from sight.
The clouds turn the color of the orioles that cry in the tree of
heaven, below which he hides,
                        eating the peaches of heaven.
The concubine beaten to death. Her body left out like that.

                         With the branch of a litchee.

With the branch of a litchee.
With the branch of a litchee.
With the branch of a litchee.
With the branch of a litchee.
With the branch of a litchee
With the branch of a litchee.
With the branch of a litchee.
With the branch of a litchee.
With the branch of a litchee.
With the branch of a litchee.

In letters I spell everything I know about
spelling the word love

My characters seem all wrong
I write
"I'm sorry" again

What do we care for? Our "characters seem all wrong"?
Without their bedding

I would know your sheets warm, love,
I would risk your soft as snow.

Because I'd seen them so often come here
to the most remote part of the garden and rub the centers

of their bodies together beneath their changing petals,
I considered them part of my own. And they considered me the same

coming to me as they did on this day.
They took one of my fruit and gave it to her, and then taking my

branch and stripping it of all its leaves,
and stripping her garments, they beat her with my branch,

the white flesh of my fruit running through her fisted hand until it
      held only my seed.

If it is true, as the lemons say, that he is a god, then this must
be the way it is done. I saw her stiffen, from blossom to dead

       and pregnant fruit, the white flesh almost beaten away, her
body rolled to a ball.

I saw a kind of shell within her open, its contents taken by the wind.
       Ah, so this is how they are borne.

Why I Slept with Him

Let me tell you a story. A woman farmer had two she-goats.
Mornings, her old spine hurt her

                    and the scar across her back

sang as if missing limbs. "Ready, willing, and petrified," she might
have said, scattering the ends among the chickens.

Springs before she'd left off milking,
she always had a few kids

                    hopping in the yard like cupids.
The billy she penned separately so the milk wouldn't taste like sex.
Then, death approached with the rustic

twittering of juncos, the place a shambles, the tree rats

                              deep in the brush.

I know nothing
        of goats. I apologize beforehand that they become tangled in
my story. The billy will wish it'd never had horns,

                            its whole life spent
licking its own penis and scratching those castles on its head
as if they were boils that needed lancing;

the she-goats will be in chains, put on a run by a well meaning city-
man who will sit on his newly acquired front porch
and wonder at

                    a jug of milk and crisp cherries
and how goats have short tails and sheep, long.

Tethered too closely together cleaning the city-man's brush

the she-goats will become tangled,
like a bad marriage, the city-man will think.
In the evenings he will untangle them — See? How he pulls
the black one's leg from the chain about the little

one's neck in the moon light? And how, understanding goats as
social animals, he will inevitably run them
                                                                out again the next day?
a single rope through both their collars,
and set them close again, and here they will continue to munch

the brush until it's clear, the tree rats and juncos
                                                squeaking about the patch no longer.

Look now, it's the next day, he's done as we thought he would.

It's evening. Let's go down and untangle them.
                                                We'll take their places.
Here he is with his well meaning hands.
The pupils of our eyes are sliced off at the top and the bottom
and we've lost our voices. Have you ever seen how sad
                                                a goat's eyes are? Look into mine.

As he runs us back, we notice the billy lying dazed
on the ground
with blood where its testicles were,
                                                and how well cut the south field is.
Now that I've come to the end, you will want me to say
                                                which life I want to lead.

The Celery Cutters' Song

We talked in the celery about the Russian
Jews with what little we knew, about the human
tendency to shtetls, our arms and hands dotted
with the yellow blotches, our boots, pants and nails dirtied.
Love and laziness singing at the periphery,
                              we spoke on, the celery

often calling us to silence. Mansions bordered
us from three sides. We searched for any order
where we could hang our words, and though we spoke and worked
from dawn that morning, filling every crate we brought,
that other song, *her legs so white*, grew. Sipping tea,
                              we talked in the celery

as we lunched, chewing the acrid leaves. Is there harm,
is it wrong, to wonder at lives like they are poems?
The truck came. We piled on the wormy and yellowed
ones for the goats and then the crates. The sky changed.
The song returned. We watched and rode the bed, silently,
                              we, in the truck with the celery.

PART III

After Words

Here is a wall. The strange empty space above the wall . . . what is it for? Here, a little boat, a canopy of silver plastic rattling above it.

Listen to the babe-scare cry of the wind. You are in the unsteady boat and this poem is a lake.

It's too late now. You are in the boat my little skipperoo, my kitzie koodle. Look. In the other boat, your son. All the rest, the other sons, the boy you blinded and the daughter you maimed, the weapons and the armor, is film, a thin and punctured membrane, a fictitious hymen.

There's no place for that weapon here. Come on now, you have no choice. Trust me.

I'll speak nonsense. You speak truth. We'll see what comes of it.

The Carpenter

The peacock is so extravagant
His cry so open
His form so forgiven
God, what else could a man or woman
       want than to be the blessed inhabitant

Of such a body. To have milled the boards
       for its housing. Hemlock no less,
       what a piece of work, the peacock's
       floors are all tongue and groove.

To have stood on that roof
And glimpsed, hammer in hand, as he stepped
       from his robes into the bath
       they had drawn for him, what feeling
I had!
       I crashed through the skylight as if it were thatch.
I came down as if I were the god hatched
From heaven, breaking through the ceiling.
He stood there amid the glass and touched my head

       his eyes empty like those of a deer
       his legs like freshly planed pine, his mouth opening
       but then closed.
I shook violently, and as my vision began to fade
He turned his wet feet and pattered away.

This perfect boy who drew me to the ground
       returned to his bath unopposed.

The Bird

A bird loved me. We met over a small lake. It was
sleeping like a country boy, head

between the knees, not like a bird at all.

Neither the water below nor the leaves

were as green.

I watched it, and when the chance came I chased it on
the ground and caught it

as though it were a chicken in the yard.

Like a child, I must handle what I love. In my hands it became
mesmerized. I'm not sure if from fear or wonder.

The next day it spoke. It had put on clothes.

We talked long hours about the avian

and the humane. It admitted the clothes were uncomfortable,
particularly

at night. It was shy. We lived like this for some days.

I left.

After a time, I willed myself into a small bird.

Then a larger one. A night bird, a day
bird. Until I was just right, just its size.

And this is how you've found me.

One bird, one,
and a cord
of twisted hair

Death and a Fig

We'll eat figs, dried, black figs,
while it rains outside, while it rains
through the doors and windows.
There will be very little speaking
during the meal, mostly tasting and forks
clinking, footsteps going from the table
to the kitchen for more. We'll say
wasps

And when there's some rice
on the mouth of a mouth-severed fig
we'll say *wasp eggs*

Model of a Tree Growing in the Path of a Spiral

If a tree were to grow in a spiral path, each leaf coming only from the main trunk, the trunk traveling in a circuitous manner to maximize the area of leaf to sun's light, maintaining an equivalent mass to trees of the branching figure type, this tree would no doubt be of spherical dimensions. In order to support its own weight—once it had completed its first arches, having grown to sufficient height to lean over and touch its head to the ground: growing along the ground then for a period, until, once again, skyward and leaning over, the pliant trunk crosses itself; completing in this manner groin after groin until a sort of vault appears (a contour drawing where the instrument never leaves the marking surface)—the tree must not only cross itself over innumerable times through the span of its life, but will eventually graft to itself at these points, thereby increasing the efficiency of nutrient transport from its asymmetrically spiraling root mass (the root does not derive its energy from a single radiating source, nor need it contend with gravity in an unsupportive medium). As this network of intersecting arches we will still call a tree (its leaves appearing and disappearing with the seasons) adds cambium, layer upon layer, as the earth slides and slides on its ellipse, the spaces between this tree's junctures will diminish until, finally, the tree forms itself into a perfect hemisphere. And in the middle of this hemisphere, let there live a hen of fanned tails, and on each tail let there be an unblinking eye.

Immuenoa

Mediaeval venture capitalists — Guelfs of Genoa,
Loyal to the papacy — sent out in coastal galleys
Vaguely Homeric bands of men onto the ocean sea,
And south, along the western coast of Africa. Their call,

Immuenoa, rumored flower, its root milk said to sweeten
The very soil that bore it — men savored even the dirt
Clods that dangled from its root. The Islands off Cabo
Verde, in Ptolemy's obscure chartings called *Fortunatae*

Insulae, or the *Hesperides*, westernmost of lands
Below the movement of the sun, could save the Holy
Republic from ruin, and would: with these vessels Reason
Had deemed in its stern but bleeding heart to meet

The flower with Rome, as goats grazed on the Capitol,
And cows lowed speeches on the wealth of grasses in the Forum.

PART IV

As in *Bedtime for Bonzo*

The cuckoo drops its eggs in another's nest.

Blue

A row of shelves hides a wall and a door here. They are all blue,
    just blue.

I wonder if you and I would ever paint a wall together, and a door.
      Take one color and paint it all, even the hinges and the knob.

And then each other, clothes and all.
      Just some color to put on history, not to change it, but to look

at it together and remember what we did to what we see
                          over what we cannot see.

Note from the Plagiarist

That winter, I reread the book in the library where, I later learned, the author himself had often sat and read, in the town where he died. I was searching for a poem that spoke of work to give to a friend's husband, a carpenter. But, perhaps insensitively, I also meant it for her, a kind of apology. She was afraid I had plagiarized one of her poems, or, at least, gutted it and then reused the guts. When she reminded me of her work, I was afraid also: the same blue door, its knob, its hinges.

In that book I found the king salmon, and the fishes coming out of its mouth. The eels, I already knew, were his, though it took months to place them. But the fish as well, they too had come from him. I realized my life, even its weaker sentiments, had been written for me, almost as if planned: the poem about work, it wasn't in the book. Yet, months before, as I sat in a real chair and wrote to you, I saw a door hidden behind shelves, its hinges, blue.

Water and Earth

The Blouse

Film of my life, draped across my shoulders, do not rip, do not
catch on an offending
branch as I lift you above my knees and cross this cunning river.

On the other side lies a fruit I must have though it
stain you, your hem in my fingers, your folds now a pocket.

Big Elm

Mother draped coats over its main forks till it looked upholstered.

We had garbage bags of clothes hung in the higher branches.
We found occasionally suitcase-sized loaves of bread up there.
Its lowest limb had died and was cut off—The stump was covered
with studs, buttons, broken jewelry and pieces of mirror.

Friar Buck and His Dog

In the woods behind the Tang's, in whose basement I've lived
                 since the binding of my niece's feet, now five months,
where the hummock slopes toward the river.

I have dreams where all the castrated dogs play happily in a pasture.
They've tape over their cuts; still they bite and paw each other
            impassively.

The alders have taken the canopy.
You, a girl who's lived fifty-nine years,
                 lead me down a path in the moonlight.

A rusty voice translates Alfaro's prayer —
              Convince yourself, Pochocho, dear, just nothing would
           you gain being a man, and nothing would I lose being a dog.

You come out of your cave like an anchorite,
the path a rocky and curving one.

Have I submitted you to this abject life?
You, girl, shame me like seven aunts who will never marry.

Your ill-fitting dog-hair coat, patched like alder bark, your walk
                 like a raccoon's, you'd think it wasn't painful.
Look, I'm writing you in poems —

    I see an old woman, old head shorn, amble down the mountain.
She's a load on her back, a laugh like a bark. Oh, what she
                    wants to do is walk!

—as if you'd bother with them.
I used to think you obsequious.

Now I know how poor my judgment is, my brain, a poison, your
soul, a fertile sea.
Growl and snarl at me, as I stupidly walk you into the ground.

When Ronald Reagan Was a Boy

He found an abandoned motorcycle and brought it home. He tenderly rebuilt the engine with the help of Mr. Mertz, the old German bachelor who lived a mile down the way. In a month, it ran. Ron rode it to town as often as his parents would allow. On special nights like tonight, an autumn dance, he would stay out late and ride home by whatever light the sky provided. Turn off your headlights. If you wait for the blindness to pass, the road will return. You will see as Ron saw those nights on his cycle home: the faint, bobbing ghosts of white deer rumps along the roadside and then, higher, over a fence; the road white against the dark of the clover and burdock the deer must have been grazing on. Needing only that white. He never repaired the headlamp.

Rarely, when another vehicle came along, he saw in the distance its light, and pulled to the side of the road. He heard the dance in his head, the music keeping time to the drone of his engine: off the shoulder, the slight glow of the passed car's lamps still in his eyes. His cycle yelling in the high register of first gear over any other sounds of the night. The road white beneath him. Dropping into second, he finally heard the sudden, unlit chug of the oncoming engine. It clipped his shoulder with its dull, unlit side lamp as they passed. The cool of the road continued to pass around him;

the familiar light of distant houses carried him; truly, he slid through the darkness on that little engine. This was how he broke his shoulder, though he told them different.

Telling My Love the Myth of Twos

My twin takes his bow from the ground. Jaguars balanced above
    reflections in a spring

lap, tongues plunging and not plunging into the water. In this field
    everything is

in twos. Two men, two women and their shadows come into the
    grasses speaking

as they walk. *Castor and Pollux lift their lights above the horizons,*
    the elder

woman says below us. Our feet strike the ground of the sky as we
    pad across

heaven, our breath barely lifted. Daylight's hood recedes. The true
    sky comes into view.

The men and women couple in the night, resting in the grasses.
    Listen, Love, in my story

we think ourselves doubles of each other but are mistaken. Listen —
    Can you hear?

A boy in the morning, bottles of milk clinking in his bike's wire
    basket

to the inconstancy of the one wheel followed by its brother. The
    boy wakes the lovers,

the distant clatter, practicing his imitation of the jaguar's
    frightening cry to himself.

At Eagle Grief Stream the Horse
of the Will Is Held and Reined

Of the stream itself his notes say little. He reined in his horse and
looked around.

Of the village he records
      For the rest of the day we lay smoking of the daintiest portions.
Of darkness he reports
           The Day Sentinel and the Guardian.
Of the lodge his squaw gave
           A vessel of water.

Of wolves,
      A woman crouched beside an open door, beating her head
                with a stone and weeping.
Of the voyagers
         The dwelling, A dried meat they called pemmican,
            A dozen scattered children.

Of luck
    That Indians have been known to ride into the midst of an enemy's
        camp to be rid of a life supposed to lie under the heel of fate.

He mounted and rode round the village of Heaven without regard
      for good or ill.

Of faith and of mercy,
         Why did you have to use your tricks to harm me?

Pilgrim's Progress

Hsüan-tsang and his party traveled fourteen days from Ait Aein to
Wansgelt. Look. On the eighth day. Here they come:

His little monkey companion rattles its collar bell;
And the piglet requires more water than they can afford.
The little monkey's bell sounds loudly in the silent heat,
Disharmonious to the company's foot falls;
The piglet requires drink! Oh, the poor foundling piglet
Wants its paddock. Why was it taken from its mama's ninny?
At midday they lunch on tea and cookies;
                                        they nap in wait
For the day's cooler hours. The toothless horse farts, shading
Beneath the locust tree:
                    How could this nag be a long
Whiskered dragon? And this piglet, drinking all my water —
        an immortal?
The monkey jingles its bell, and points its tiny member west.

PART V

The Organum   *A Cartoon Memoir*

The Lonely Journey;
At Yellow Wind Ridge The T'ang Monk Meets Adversity

Thence we were to make the long journey to the settle.
The clouds opened at the point where they first had

The wind, and rested by the waters, who clothed
Themselves with Thee.

Trembling all over he began the Heart Sutra
(but we shall say no more of that here)
Then he stooped down and drew out of the
                                                grass by Thee.

T'ang monk away; like hawks catching sparrows

Tarry, and a wide green meadow where about forty;

The tiger down the slope of the mountain, saw
The gold cicadas casting their shells, and left his skin.

They were involved in a mantle of clouds, in restless
(motion, as if urged by strong winds.)
The monster saw them approaching. He again stripped.

"Thunder," Pilgrim cried, "What shall we do?"
Tears fell from his eyes. "Where shall we go to look?"

The two of them indeed rushed up the mountain.
The distant hills assumed strange distorted shapes in

The side of the stream, and waited there till the rage of
The torrent had passed.

There, not enough space for us to sleep, we sat beneath.

Taking French Leave

Heifers to their wagons to carry them forward upon their
Hot prairie.
Here he came to stop. Hendrick was in the shafts.

Horses were picketed in the area within; and the whole
Head of light

Hung at the side of her mule; and his pipe was slung at
Her back.

Hundreds of dogs, of all sizes and colors, ran restlessly.
Having spent half an hour there, he took his leave first.

The Big Blue;
Many Gods Try to Catch the Monster, a Rebel in Heaven

Elder brother, now I know, you are something of a crook
        and a shakedown artist.

Equal to Heaven Residence, the girls approached them,
        saying, We.
Effectually, we sat upon our saddles with faces of the ut-
(most sullenness, while the water dropped from the visors.)
End of the night, we were unconsciously reposing in
        small pools of rain,
Emperor added anxiety.

                Next came the Great Immortal of Naked
English double barreled rifle, took aim at her heart and
(discharged into it first one bullet and then another. She
was then butchered on the most approved principles of
woodcraft, and furnished a very welcome item to our
somewhat limited bill of fare.)

Each man mounting a horse, we rode through the stream
(the stray animals following of their own accord.)

The Hunting Camp;
At Eagle Grief Stream the Horse of the Will Is Held and Reined

One bird is lost,
One, and a cord
Of twisted hair,
Only when his   life is made a payment for my horse will I have
Offspring.

The T'ang Monk Escapes His Ordeal

Revenge went secretly into the meadow and gave her a
Rifle. I lost sight of him beyond the rising ground.

The Buffalo,

Gathered and parted like clouds, were surrounded by the bleak
Grass, not far off, quite lifeless, and another violent
Guard on our side of the camp, thinking it no part of his.

Getting drunk often at the Peach Feast, he woke: the moon
        shone.

Great banquet for peace in Heaven, we have little to offer.

The Frontier

A multitude of birds we overtook on our way across
       the continent,
And, not far distant,

A great ocean in the midst of which was located,
       accordingly,
A sheet iron bridge. And beyond it, a piece of heaven

Appears truly like a hanging,
A column of rising white rainbows

Atop the crimson ridges.

And all the monkeys clapped their hands in acclaim:
       "Marvelous water and earth!"

About to leave, he got on the raft himself
And taking advantage of the wind, set sail for the border
       of the south.
A strong southeast wind which lasted for days sent him
       to the north.
As it was, it was to be a long and arduous voyage
(on which the persevering reader, if he so chooses,
may accompany him)

The Ogillallah Village

Noon, we stopped by some pools of rain water.
No coming, no leaving, no parinamana,

No giving, no taking.

Naked, he knelt down and cried, "Master, I'm out."

Night's lodging below
Night's white dog.

Name, for they seemed acquainted with
Neither heat nor cold, and taking the course most
      agreeable to their

Name that signifies
Now is a good time,

Now, said he, let us go.
Now began in good earnest.

Metal and Wood, in Compassion, Rescue Little Children

"Up here,
Up to a thousand miles during the day, and even at night, they
Understand you correctly," said the old man. "You are telling
Us with a huge banquet."

"Up here and let's measure our true abilities," my dear son said,
Upon me, half in earnest and half in jest,
Unable to contain himself.

At Double-Fork Ridge, Po-ch'in Detains the Monk;
Hunting

My own exhausted strength soon gave out, so I loosed
Myself to the shore, the margin of the water, and watched
      the restless
Mountains, at a loss in what direction to go.

Muttering a monk's recitation
May our Buddha be merciful and reveal to
Myself in cleaning my rifle and pistols, and making

Meal, dusk fell, and thus
      Shadows moved to the Star River's nearing pulse;
      The moon was bright with not a speck of dust.

My little mare Pauline was soon standing by the fire.
Men, foreheads on their arms, were sleeping under the cart.

May our Buddha be merciful and soon reveal to me
(his Diamond Body sixteen feet tall.)

Morning, they went to prepare food to serve the priest,
Mounted, crossed the little stream, pushed through the trees,
Much tormented by attacks of green-headed flies.
      As I watched,

Mond rolled his eyes vacantly about,
"Many thanks! And you two, how have you behaved these

Many miles?" He clucked his tongue and drew a frown,
"'Me, great king! Save me, great

Monster king, seated up on high!' Truly!" He
Moved forward,

Muttering.
        "You do not realize, Elder," said Po-ch'in, "that

Might be heading in the wrong direction." In that very anxious
Moment, the order was given. The ogres pounced on the
(attendants like tigers preying on sheep.)

"Master has come!" Our monk was dumbfounded. Po-ch'in
(trembled. We do not know who was crying, and you must
listen to the explanation in the next)

Mountain,
        and the Guardian began to ascend it as if he were walking.

Notes

The final word in the epigraph by Basho alters the line in Nobuyuki Yuasa's translation from *The Narrow Road to the Deep North* (London, 1966). "Hototogisu" represents the Japanese cuckoo's song and also names the bird in that language.

In the seventh century the Buddhist monk Hsüan-tsang traveled from Chang-an province to India and back, a journey of fifteen years. His goal was to bring back to China knowledge in the form of key Buddhist texts. "Journey to the West," and "Event" adapt language from Anthony C. Yu's translation of the sixteenth-century novel *The Journey to the West* (author unknown, Chicago, 1977), a fictional retelling of the monk's travels. The penultimate section of "Event" was composed in collaboration with poet Sarah Perrier.

"Memories Are Nothing, Today Is Important" is dedicated to Miroslav Buljan.

"Friar Buck and His Dog": "Convince yourself . . ." these lines are translated from a poem by Mexican poet Alfredo Aguilar Alfaro (1902–1986), written to his dog Pochocho.

"Immuenoa" is dedicated to Rev. Jake Bohstedt Morrill.

"Blue" is dedicated to poet Kathy Anita Gonzales.

"At Eagle Grief Stream the Horse of the Will Is Held and Reined" and "The Organum" are wholly composed of language from Francis Parkman's *The Oregon Trail* (Boston, 1875) and from the first twenty-six chapters of *The Journey to the West*.

CPSIA information can be obtained
at www.ICGtesting.com
Printed in the USA
FSOW01n1008210416
19519FS

9 780300 102727